IN THE MUSEUM OF HUNTING AND NATURE

IN THE MUSEUM OF HUNTING AND NATURE

Cynthia Randolph

San Francisco, California

© 2023 Cynthia Randolph

All rights reserved

ISBN-13: 978-1-7374947-9-9

Cover artwork by Hilary Pecis

Author photo by Loden Simsak

San Francisco, California

for Loden

*Seeing is forgetting
the name of the thing one sees.*

Paul Valéry

*I became myself and
was haunted by it*

Mary Ruefle

CONTENTS

Preface	i
Jawbreaker	1
Sound Effects	2
Wings	3
Dark Matter	4
Dreamwork	5
Camera Obscura	6
Still Life	7
Another Time	8
Rome	9
Ghost Stories	10
A Walk in the Woods	11
I Want to Know the Name of the Bird	13
Worry	15
Labyrinthitis	16
Every Day I Miss the Sunset so I Turn Away from the Sky	20
Sea Life	21
In the Museum of Hunting and Nature	23
Window	25
Josef Albers, Homage to the Square: Guarded, 1952	26
My Life was a Beautiful Mystery on the Verge of Understanding	27
Untold Stories	29
Daylight Robbery	30
Breasts	31
An Impossible Thing is Happening in the Most Boring Setting You Can Imagine	32
The Angel	34
Mother Tongue	36
In June 2020 the Golden Gate Bridge Began to Hum	37
Hiding Place	40

The Art of Disappearance	41
The Story	43
Green	46
Numbers	48
Green Light Corridor	49
I Slipped Off	52
Gardening	53
Sky Blue Sky	55
Averted Vision	57
How to Disappear	60
Winter Greens	62
The Mirror Stage	63
9pm	68
Sleep Sound	69
Beach	71
There are Places Where the Sky Comes Closer to You	73
There are No Rules	75
The Butcher of Paris	76
Failure Fun House	77
Glass Concert	83
A Place	85
I am not Writing an Instagram Post	87
The Attic	88
Walking down Church Street at 5pm on a Monday	89
Living Room	90
Early Morning Sounds	91
Daguerreotype	92
Rebellion in Science	93
Sky Burial	94
A Lot of Sorrow	95
Notes	96
Author's Note	99
Acknowledgments	100

PREFACE: MATERIALS, REAL TEARS

Cynthia Randolph is an artist, as well as a writer. She works across photography, film, drawing, sculpture, poetry, and creative nonfiction. The title of this, her first poetry collection, references Paris' most unusual and intriguing attractions, The Museum of Hunting and Nature, where wildness reigns. Heritage weapons, taxidermy, tapestry, and trophies roam among contemporary artwork examining the codependent but often fraught relationship between humankind and the natural world. Within its walls, boundaries between the sublime and the ridiculous fall away. Each overstuffed room (from the Cabinet of the Wolf to the Salon of the Dogs) is an ode to exuberant maximalism. There, Randolph finds a woman's bust that can cry forever.

It's intriguing to contrast this more-is-more eclecticism with the restraint that characterizes Randolph's own creative output. Her visual artwork is precise, elegant, and controlled. Her poems similarly respect the power of clean geometry and economy of expression. In both realms, she mirrors the minimalism and repetitive patterning of composers like Phillip Glass and Terry Riley. Randolph has several ekphrastic poems in this collection, one of which contains the title of the painting that inspired it: "Homage to the Square: Guarded, 1952", by Josef Albers. Albers attained maximum effect with minimal media. Randolph does the same. Her museography achieves its impact with an almost scientific sense of exactly which elements to reveal and which to hold back, such that the reader has the sensation of encountering a purified essence with each poem.

Randolph's refined imagery concentrates our field of vision. In "Dream" the narrator recounts:

At the end of one alleyway
there is a hole of light from the above. Let's go
back, I say..... You go to the above. I go to the hole of light.

Lines from a poem about her mother "Sky Burial" considers a different form of camera obscura:

*I wanted to roll out a field of sunprint paper
and on it place each object, each thrift store
trinket, what remained. I wanted to watch
the sun burn in a memory of them
bury them in the light*

The poet-filmmaker is sensitive to the notion of aperture and perspective. In imagery and in meter, time itself can be compressed, extended, erased, dissolved, sped up, and paused. She defines and employs principles of averted vision and persistence of vision. She asks:

*is too much light
just another form
of blindness?*

These lens adjustments are essential to focusing the imagination. In a poem about the common house sparrow, she queries:

*why do we love what is rare
and despise what is all around us*

As readers, we have the choice to debate answers to this question or we can acknowledge that one of poetry's gifts is its ability to elevate the everyday to the realm of rarity and, conversely, to align the intimate with unifying truths about the human condition. Throughout this beautiful and affecting collection, Randolph metaphorically employs the physical actions captured in her own poems. She presses thoughts through a sieve. She rubs with ever-decreasing grits of sandpaper. She digs and digs. As a result, she captures both the mundane and the profound and decocts them into line, forms, and sensation. Like the jawbreaker passed between two people over the course of eight and a half hours in the opening poem (which is based on her video performance piece) what remains at the end is silence. And the memory of the exchange – a sweetness shared.

Tamsin Spencer Smith
San Francisco, CA

JAWBREAKER

In the beginning
there was a very big ball
of sugar
between them
they ate through it
little by little
it was very loud
it took a long time
it was very sweet
sickeningly so
they ate it all
in the end
there was nothing
between them
it was very quiet

SOUND EFFECTS

A subliminal collage of sound
threads in and out
distant insane laughter
slamming iron doors
a bleating animal cry
then another sound
much nearer
the scrape of something across slate
the sound of tiny hooves suddenly
turns into the rattle of distant rain
then changes abruptly to a speeding sedan
then a terrible scriiitching sound
of locks falling shut
over the sounds of lovemaking
and the twilight zone sound
of running footsteps
and your father's voice
faint at first
then echoed
a million miles away
cross-fading
birds singing
children playing
expanding the simple tune
to symphonic boundless dimensions
the little girls fade
into thin air
we fade
to black

WINGS

The second summer of college, in an effort to pursue my own passions, I gave up a comparatively well-paying paralegal position to work as an assistant for an artist, a job which entailed waking up extremely early to sand a large chunk of leftover Lincoln Memorial marble with ever-decreasing grits of sandpaper, outside, in the sun, and sometimes the rain. It was, the marble was, eventually, the shape of a large wing. A human-sized wing. Over time, by the end, it shined. It was to be in an exhibit with Louise Bourgeois' Spider, of which I had no concept. Not its existence. Nor its importance. I only remember the sanding. And my fingers, also sanded. And my arms, their lean tone by the end. The conversations in hushed voices over the marble, and the sound of sanding. The endless sound of sanding. Black boxes appeared at the gallery during the installation, hundreds of yellow tiger swallowtail butterflies, which we pinned to the walls behind the wing, and around the corner, dipping slightly towards the black spider-filled room. After the opening, all around the large white marble wing, scattered all over the floor, were hundreds of wings, half wings, their bright yellow powder lightly covering everything.

DARK MATTER

You told me I should
write a poem about dark matter
and because you are ten
I know you mean the kind
that is in your big book about space
how am I supposed to
write about something so big
write about something I can not explain
write about something I do not understand
no one can
no one can
even explain
how the Jacaranda trees
with their purple
petaled messes
have memories
communicate pain
each night
I hold your small hand
in the dark
and think about dark matter
not the kind in your big book about space
the other kind

DREAMWORK

We are underground walking through the empty streets of a buried city with hundreds of doorways. I stop at each one and photograph it. Look, I say. Some doorways have gates. Some have shutters. The light leaks through in quiet lines on the sidewalk. It is early. At the end of one alleyway there is a hole of light from the above. Let's go back, I say. You say nothing and try to scale the wall. The wall crumbles with your touch. The earth falls inwards. You keep trying. The earth keeps falling. You go to the above. I go to the hole of light. I ask if I could also get there. Yes, you say, looking down. Then there is only silence. And the hole of light. To the silence I ask, what is prayer?

CAMERA OBSCURA

The photography teacher
took us into a room
where there was no light
we sat in the silent dark
while our eyes adjusted
he pierced a small hole
in the shade
on the wall opposite
the prick of light
the entire cathedral appeared
upside down
saturated with color
the gargoyles in perfect focus
the rain outside
falling upward

STILL LIFE

Do you believe a place changes
by the sounds that have occupied it?
I do. Even if it is not scientifically sound
today I very much want to somehow escape
the black mirror constant notification cycle
to be muted, to hear only presence
room tone, the ambient sound
of a space captured by sound
artists at the end of shoot
the sound that is and isn't silence
where there is no dialogue
sound between sound
which cannot be faked
probably like there is right now
as you are reading these words
shifting in your chair
dampened faraway sounds
a car on your street, the wind
I want field recordings of everyone I know
in their specific silence
the silences that surrounded me as a child
the faint sound of eggbeaters
mixing batter rooms away
the muffled deep hollow sound of arguing
while tucked beneath a canopy of white
Victorians covered their mirrors with white cloth
the distracting reflections
known to hide ghosts
and memories of earthly things
things we and the dead
are trying to forget

ANOTHER TIME

I imagine
every single playground
stitched together
in a single photograph
in it is the longest swing set
ever seen
the wind ghosts
of children
playing

ROME

In the photography exhibition
that wrapped its one hundred photographs
around the entire gallery
its one hundred portraits
of people each year of life
I saw my son
lingering at the end
staring up
at the wrinkled face
of a stranger
a century of experience
etched into her skin
I realized then
in a way I had not before
one day I would die
and he would live

GHOST STORIES

In the modern dictionary
of all of our new
horrifying behaviors
haunting is defined
as someone who tries
to contact you
after they have vanished
without word
hello. again
but hasn't haunting
always been this way?
at night
do you feel
their touch?
can you hear
their whispers?
I do
I can
Remember me!
Remember me!
chant the billion wicked thoughts
hand wringing
in my hallways
tracing my shadows

A WALK IN THE WOODS

You know
if we're going to walk
through the woods
we need a little path
let's build us a happy little path
we're just gonna take the knife
and let this path
sort of just wander
play and have fun
now we need to highlight that path
where the sun's sparkling through
there we go, there we go
now maybe, maybe,
maybe as we're walking
through the woods
maybe it rained last night
you know after it rains
you always have little rain puddles
in our world
you can do anything
I'll teach you to see
things that have been there
all your life
things you never noticed
okay, I talk too much sometimes
so we'll go back
while I have the knife here
I'm gonna take it
and just cut
what we're doing is
just literally cutting
right through

the distance
the illusion
we needed the dark
to show the light
(slow acoustic guitar)

I WANT TO KNOW THE NAME OF THE BIRD

The one that sings
the song of many notes
his song is loud
in the mute winter landscape
four strong notes
break into a flutter
of laughter
and seem to end in a question
I find him in the silhouette
of a fuchsia Bougainvillea mess
small and striped, brown
soft gray mourning doves sit on the wire
their wings make a loud whistling
as they fly away
inside I listen
to the sparrow's song online
some say they hear the first four notes
of Ludwig van Beethoven's Symphony No. 5.
in his song, I don't
in the spring
when the whole world was silenced
the sparrows' song grew more complex
they invented a new tune
they stopped straining
to have their voices heard
over all of our noise
I hear the parrots of Telegraph Hill
pass overhead
the sparrow copies the sounds
of the neighboring birds
in this way she moves in in secret
outside I help my husband

raise the first wall of my writing studio
I hold the wooden beams in place
as he secures them
a window
from nothing to nothing

WORRY

The china doll has little white hands and a blue blouse with three-quarter sleeves. In bed at night she feels her arms, their bonelessness. Her legs too are just balloon pants. No knees. Just little china feet. No shoes. The little girl holds the china doll's limp body to her own warm small body and tucks her inside the blankets. All through the night, her little china hands clink against her little china head. Always she is worried she will break her head right open that way. Nothing inside.

LABYRINTHITIS

Two children spin on a path in the woods.

↻

Sometimes I think of spinning and the spinning starts.

↻

Sometimes I think of you and the spinning starts.

↻

When the muni train hit my car, I spun across the road and hit my head. This is when I blacked out. This is when the other spinning started.

↻

I lie still on the table like a bug pinned to a mat while the doctor sticks his needles into my body. To stop the spinning. To keep the spinning stopped.

↻

What is vertigo? asks somebody. It is Labrynthitis, I say, which is what the doctor said. What is Labyrinthitis? I ask the doctor. It is the spinning, he says.

↻

I walk through airports that never end in flight and ride bicycles in circles and worry about what I am leaving behind.

↻

And yes, I am aware that the mind is inside the body and the vestibular system is inside the head and the brain is inside the mind and the body is inside the universe and everything and everyone everywhere is always spinning.

↻

What is vertigo? asks Milan Kundera. It is the voice of the emptiness below

↻

Sometimes I wonder if I spent too many years trying to live too many lives simultaneously.

☾

After a hike, I lay on my bed beneath a twenty five pound weighted blanket. I closed the door. I closed the blinds. I closed my eyes.

☾

I float.

☾

A room full of feathers, full of loft. All pillows and softness and white. There is no up. No down. No fear of falling. No fear of the voice of the emptiness below.

☾

No fear of the emptiness below. The octopuses crawl along the shore for their nightly pilgrimage from the ocean to no one knows where. Or why.

EVERY DAY I MISS THE SUNSET SO I TURN AWAY FROM THE SKY

It is dusk it is dawn it is dusk I turn my back
on the world for a little while I want to stay
here I can not stay here I keep my coat on
the night is tired of being beautiful the moon
hangs above my head like a hook as I try
to walk away from where you are I receive
messages but do not respond I dress in black
to disappear into the night but the night sky
is blue the sky is not blue says the scientist
who then says many words like light and color
and scatter blue words hang in my mouth
I want to stay here I can not stay here I keep
my coat on the stars turn their back on the world
for a little while

SEA LIFE

The announcer says they train the sea lions using operant conditioning while tossing fish after fish into the sea lion's mouth. She says they reward positive behavior and ignore bad behavior. She teaches the audience the gesture to make the sea lions stick out their tongues. *On the count of three, we are all going to give a thumbs-up,* she says in a voice that makes me believe she has more happiness than I do. The audience raises their arms and gives a thumbs-up. The sea lion opens her mouth but does not stick out her tongue. The announcer says again, in her happy voice, *On the count of three, we are all going to give a thumbs-up.* The audience holds up their thumbs. The announcer sticks out her tongue at the sea lion. The sea lion sticks out her tongue at the announcer.

Everyone is smiling. Everyone wears shorts. Everyone is on vacation. The sun is hot. It is midday.

In the row ahead of me, everyone is holding up their screens filming the quiet water. The announcer appears and introduces the three dolphins, as well as a dolphin that is half false killer whale, which she mentions was born in captivity, and is the only of her kind. She says she is a wolphin. Everyone laughs. The dolphins do flips and throw basketballs into the air. Everyone watches through the glass on their phones. One person is live streaming. The music stops and the announcer says something about plastic and dolphin-safe tuna. The music begins again and the trainer balances on the back of a dolphin and races around the pool. A mother and father hold up their phones to film it. The child between them says, looking up at them, *Let me see. Let me see.*

The father looks at his daughter, who is maybe two, and says, *You're getting sunburned. Your face is red. You need to put on sunscreen.* He pulls out a bottle of sunscreen and begins to spray it on her, saying quickly, *Close your eyes. Close your eyes.* She closes her eyes and opens her mouth. He says, *Close your eyes. Close your eyes*, in a loud voice, and keeps spraying. Her mouth is open wide. She begins to cry. He keeps spraying. *Close your eyes. Close your eyes.*

IN THE MUSEUM OF HUNTING AND NATURE

There is a perfect pure white bust of a young woman, a kind of fountain, tears pouring from her eyes, falling into a pool below. The title card reads, *Pleureuse*, *Crying Woman*. Materials, Real Tears.

I write the artist who made the Crying Woman, Serena Carone, to ask how she acquired so many real tears

she writes back

Inside the head there is a little aquarium pump that brings the water from the plate up into the eyes so she can cry forever! Have a nice day. Serena

I linger on the exclamation point

and the little aquarium pump in her head

and the *so she can cry forever*

she wanted her to cry, but not necessarily be sad

forever

last summer I had a condition where I could not stop weeping

my ophthalmologist said nothing could be done

and diagnosed me with Epiphora

which he said meant *too many tears*

tears streamed down my face continually

I had to carry a handkerchief

and apologize all of the time

and say that I was fine

I wore dark glasses

like a widow

mourning nothing

maybe everything

I imagine all of those tears pouring from my eyes because of a little aquarium pump in my head

then falling into a white porcelain bowl in my lap

Crying Woman

how did you acquire so many real tears?

WINDOW

Outside I hear
the occasional dull thud
of a mango
dropping to the ground
it is dark
the crickets are loud
the large palm fronds
in the light wind
sound like someone
opening heavy curtains
that do not exist

JOSEF ALBERS, HOMAGE TO THE SQUARE: GUARDED, 1952

Pink inside pink inside pink inside tell me their names (I should not ask these things) a house interior rooms a house exterior rooms we have rooms Jung thought this did Albers think this world inside the world inside the world inside the world let me in I cry my mother never did soft spoken apparition (I should not ask these things) outside her house ringing the bell little girl shaded green with rays no answer ran away this one beaming this one ascending bouncy ball pink storm drain grey come back grey stay he doesn't let me in (who is he I should not say) black box inside black box inside black inside black stacked then sinking then falling away

MY LIFE WAS A BEAUTIFUL MYSTERY ON THE VERGE OF UNDERSTANDING

Do you need a plan?

asks the blue insurance website page

find a plan instructs a blue button

find a plan instructs another blue button

I virtually choose

cards from a tarot card deck

ask quiet questions

my inside my head voice

transmutes each word

as it appears

which plan is the right one

becomes do we get what we deserve

over a long dry path along the coast

the Ace of Wands appears

hand reaching out of the mist

I keep picking cards

why should there be a limit to desire?

find a plan instructs the limit to my desire

UNTOLD STORIES

And the red haired child pours his marbles down the marble run for hours and the auburn haired child reads his graphic novel held up in front of his face like a large shield between him and his parents and the father drinks a beer called untold stories and the mother drinks untold stories and the children drink untold stories and they all pour untold stories into their bodies and they all pour untold stories out of their eyes and they all pour untold stories into the sink and the untold stories flow through the pipes for miles and miles out into the ocean and that is where they live.

DAYLIGHT ROBBERY

I sit in a yellowed silence
in the memory of the sound
of children singing
imagining the yellowest yellow
like bouncing around inside
a bouncy house that is a buttercup
a therapist once told me to buy a yellow sweater
that people would smile seeing it, seeing me
and to my surprise it worked
but only amplified my sadness
yellow is a difficult color
once I painted a room so yellow
its name was yellow
it took weeks to paint
the gray kept leaking through
sometimes I wonder
when people bricked up their windows
to avoid paying the window tax
did they miss the sunlight?
was the extra money
worth it?

BREASTS

In the basement of my boyfriend's mother's house, I had a small art studio space while we took care of her after a car accident where she was T-boned by a drunk driver and broke both her legs, and also her arms. For months she couldn't dress or bathe or feed herself without our help. I made many things in that windowless basement space, many of which were cement casts of my breasts. They were large heavy squares of cement that sloped upwards to the nipple. There had to be hundreds of them by the time I finally moved away. I would go down each evening after dinner and work. They were, the breast casts were, laid out in a grid, like tiles. I wanted to cover the entire floor. I wanted to grout them into place in some venue so that from afar they became a field of undulating forms. I cringe thinking of this very young art piece. I have no pictures of it. We broke up before I could take any. I tell myself that most female sculptors have a breast piece somewhere in their pasts. Look at Louise Bourgeois! And Hannah Wilke. Jenny Seville. We remained very close for many years. Best friends is what I may have called us then. He was supposed to be in my wedding, but backed out with no explanation at the last minute, then disappeared. His mother no longer lives in that house. Someone, most likely the ex maybe along with his younger brother, had to carry each one of those heavy cement breast tiles up a flight of stairs, one by one, then down another, then (somehow) get rid of them. Or maybe he kept them.

AN IMPOSSIBLE THING IS HAPPENING IN THE MOST BORING SETTING YOU CAN IMAGINE

You have probably been surrounded
by house sparrows
your entire life
house sparrows
have been seen
feeding on the 80th floor
of the Empire State Building
they have been spotted
breeding 2,000 feet underground
in a mine in Yorkshire
small brown bird
brown-winged rat
shrill, monotonous, noisy
describes their song
by the Audubon Society
which goes on to say
it's okay
to dislike some birds
birdist rule #72
why do we love what is rare
and despise what is all around us
when Eugene Schieffelin shipped the birds
in cages across the vast ocean
thinking he knew best
how to control the linden moth
and whatever other bugs
were abhorred in 1851
what were just 16
became 540 million
did he feel triumphant
when he introduced every single bird
mentioned in Shakespeare's plays

to Central Park
and how does he feel now
Shakespeare, that is, looking down
at the crop damage and disease
caused by his off-hand avian references
there's a special providence
in the fall of a sparrow
I whisper into the microphone
something about the snow
falling silently
behind the others
on the screen
something about the sparrows
I see
in their hair

THE ANGEL

In the fifth grade
I made an angel

I was proud of her wings
which were oversized

for her small body
and made her look much more

like a butterfly
I was not good at faces

so I gave her eyes
that were closed

just faint crescents
with lashes. She is asleep

I said looking up at the teacher
who had a red smock

with little yellow flowers
a sleeping angel

maybe you should make her
into a pillow

she said looking down
I stared at the angel

I had drawn on the large paper
and could not imagine

her wanting to become a pillow
but the next class

she had somehow become
drawn onto fabric

and so I stitched
her wings and I stitched

her eyelashes and I stuffed
her with cotton and she became

a pillow
I placed her on the bed

in my mother's house
before she disappeared

MOTHER TONGUE

She translates her thoughts into another language. She writes down the translation in her another language diary. She translates her translated into another language thoughts into her mother tongue. She writes down the translation in her mother tongue diary. She is now keeping two diaries. They are the same they are different they are the same. She is also taking notes. Her notes are in her mother tongue. Her thoughts are pressed through a sieve and another sieve and another sieve and on and on.

IN JUNE 2020 THE GOLDEN GATE BRIDGE BEGAN TO HUM

                                                                        June 12

The bridge is humming.

No one knows how to stop it.

                                                                         August 13

The humming is loud tonight.

The humming can be heard for miles.

                                                                     December 14

Some call it singing.
Some call it screeching.
Some call it a ghostly harmonica.
Some call it chanting monks.
Some call it a wheezing kazoo.
Some say it sounds like a noise that is used to torture prisoners.

Some want the singing to stop.

                                                                     December 15

Tonight the monks are chanting outside in the rain.

Look! The trees are singing too.

December 16

Today I tried again to understand what a non-fungible token is, and almost believed I understood finally that it is actually nothing until I learned that the nothing it is is burning through the same amount of fossil fuel as the entire country of Argentina.

Somewhere the forests of machines safekeeping nothing are humming.

December 17

It is 5am. It is still dark outside. Most lights in the houses I can see in the city are still dark. The heat just turned on. I hear the cats cleaning themselves at the foot of the bed. I hear my son across the hall breathing in his sleep.

It is nearly 7am. The sky is various shades of mauve. The lights in the houses are beginning to come on now. My son will wake up soon.

December 18

On the days when the wind blows just right it sounds like a Mongolian throat singer.

A team of acoustic and aerodynamic engineers in Ontario is working furiously to figure out how to make the humming stop.

December 19

Bridge officials found the singing often matches the musical note A.

"A" is generally used as a standard for tuning. Every string instrument in the orchestra has an A string. When the orchestra tunes, the oboe plays an "A" and the rest of the instruments tune to match that pitch.

Some want the A to stop. And the singing to stop. And the humming to stop. And the kazoo to stop. And the chanting monks to stop.

December 20

And the ghosts to stop.

December 21

It has taken me some time to admit how much I miss you.

HIDING PLACE

I used to hide
in the bottom
shelf of the bookcase
back
back
back
I pushed myself
and replaced each book
one by one
I used to hide
in the trees
I used to hide
under the covers
I used to hide
in a room
much like this one
I am hiding
now
I am hiding
inside
this
poem

THE ART OF DISAPPEARANCE

I said I need time
to be alone

(poof!)
I went away

for a few days
now I am

alone
I want to be back

but I am
staying here

since I said
this is what I want

I told a friend
and they sent me

The Art of Disappearance
an article

I am listening to
as I walk

through this city
I know well

but where
my friends are all away

Attende! Attende!
says the woman

pulling the leash back
on her dog

the leaves have begun
to accumulate

along the canal
pain

means bread in French
I see it everywhere

THE STORY

On the porch swing, the girl reads
the story of Madeleine to the sister of
                      Noah. Inside the adults are talking.
Inside the adults are eating. The sister of
                      Noah brings another book to the girl
to read on the porch swing. The girl reads
the story of Madeleine to the sister of
                      Noah. Inside the adults are talking.
Inside the adults are eating. Madeleine lives
in an old house in Paris covered in vines.
The sister of
                      Noah lives in a great grey house
with a trellis of roses. Inside the girl traces her finger
over two initials carved into the sill of the window.
Inside the girl traces her finger around a heart
carved around the two initials. The sister of
                      Noah brings the girl another book
to read. On the porch swing
the girl reads the story of Madeleine to the sister of
                      Noah.
Inside the adults are talking.
Inside the adults are eating.
The Rabbi says
                      Noah will always be young.
His eyes will always be bright.
His heart will never grow bitter.
Stop it! Stop it! says the sister of

                Noah.
First with her red face. Then with her eyes.
Then with her voice.
Out loud. The parents of the sister of
                Noah are crying.
The mother of the sister of
                Noah says she is sorry.
The mother of the sister of
                Noah
says she is sorry again.
Everyone says they are sorry.
Mostly with their eyes.
The sister of
                Noah says *Stop It!*
with her eyes.
The sister of
                Noah walks away.
The sister of
                Noah brings the girl another book.
On the porch swing the girl reads
the story of Madeleine
to the sister of
                Noah.
Inside the adults are talking.
Inside the adults are eating.
Inside everyone is taking turns
crying. Mostly with their eyes.
Sometimes with their voices.
Inside everyone is taking turns

saying they are sorry.
Mostly with their eyes.
Sometimes with their voices.
Mostly with their eyes.
The sister of
                    Noah brings the girl another book.
On the porch swing
the girl reads
the story
of Madeleine
to the sister of
                    Noah.

GREEN

I pour olive green
into the center and wrap

my arms around the
circumference, so I can

swirl the glaze around, coating
the entire platter with a thick green

that will become turquoise
at 2300 degrees, I realize

I have no ability to express
whatever it is that I am

doing or feeling
in French, but also in English

It feels good
to be freed from language

for a little while. My thoughts
are simple. I am swirling

this way. I am swirling
that way. Almost

to the edge. Follow
the line. Make the curve

pleasant. And then
there are no thoughts. Just

staring at the green pool
hugging a platter

in the back of an empty
studio, under a little light.

NUMBERS

How old is your mother? asks the white piece of paper on the clipboard. I wonder how old my mother is. I can no longer remember an age. Or even a last birthday. She is zero is the only thing I can think to write, so I write zero. I change the zero to infinity instead and move on to the next question. I am late. The doctor will see me, but I will have to wait until she has seen all of the other patients who were on time. In the waiting room, everyone is pregnant. How many children do you have? One I think. I write one. But maybe they mean pregnancies. In that case I mean four. I write four. But maybe they mean healthy pregnancies, in which case I mean three. I write three. I've only had one miscarriage if that's what they're asking. I write one. I cross out only. So much blood, I write. I wanted to have two children is what they want me to write. So I write, I wanted to have two children. I wanted to have four children. I wanted to have a house full of children. I wanted to have too many children. I wanted to be the old woman who lives in a shoe. I wanted to have more children. I write one again. The erasures make the paper gray and uneven below the number one, which seems more right, more accurate.

GREEN LIGHT CORRIDOR

The poet said she hates the color green I am sorry to tell you that I have green eyes and yes they are recessive and also my son's name is Loden which is a name that came to me in a dream a week before he was helped out of my body by my Dr. Green who has been my ob/gyn since I was 23 when I had a miscarriage a few years ago I needed a D&C the anesthesiologist's name was also Dr. Greene Green with an e strangely to me even then I thought as I counted backwards inhaling laughing gas Dr. Green and Dr. Greene will make me unpregnant now since my body will not let go of what might have been the restaurant where we had our wedding reception was Viridian its name and also the color of its walls the photographer took pictures against what was supposed to be a deep green backdrop but was instead the exact shade of green screen green which is HEX COLOR #00B140 in front of it everyone pretended to be someplace else my entire wedding party squeezed into the frame and held their breath pretending to be underwater I never made a wedding album I never   could   choose   the photographs out of   the thousands she took I never superimposed the green screen images onto anything else they are somewhere inside a green linen box now should I go on my therapist's office is on Green Street in 1969 the artist Bruce Nauman began making corridors in 1970 he made a work he titled Green Light Corridor where you are forced to turn sideways and shuffle along through his 1 foot wide 40 foot long hallway where the walls are pressed so close together that they touch both your front and your back forcing your head to choose whether to turn to face forwards or backwards as you navigate what feels like the walls closing in on you saturated from above by dense green fluorescent light in 2016 the city of Detroit launched a program they called Green Light Corridor where they put high definition cameras everwhere so they could watch crimes unfold in real time with the use of round the clock surveillance I still wonder if anyone on the naming committee knew Nauman's work I can't say but in a window next to this window I am looking online at an image of a woman pressed into Nauman's corridor she looks stuck it reminds me of a book of fairies I saw once when I was small how they were pressed so tightly into the book that they looked as if they were pressed like flowers in a flower press I wasn't allowed to buy the book but still think of it sometimes I think of the first time I saw the Wizard of Oz and did not understand the part where the green curtain is pulled back at all the apartment I stayed in in Paris this past summer had a large green door with a large green knob in the center of it after you squeeze yourself through the Green Light Corridor for some time the whole world turns a bright bright magenta

I SLIPPED OFF

my wedding ring
and dropped it
into the small
red biohazard bag
when we go
under as they say
where does the soul go
I am not asking
hypothetically
when we sleep
do we leave our bodies
for days after
my artificial absence
I was caught
between sleep and dream
wondering if I could visit
the library
of all of the selves
I have
ever been

GARDENING

All day I have been trying
to get to the root of it
and I don't mean just the ivy
that has made its way
over the fence
into my garden
wrapping
its dumb
thick
hooked
vines
around my plants
it is also
the jasmine
spiraling
its stupid
tendrils
around my sword ferns
strangling them
more
tightly
every
day
wafting
its sickeningly sweet
fragrance
all over the place
I have been trying
to be good
I have
I really have
I have been

digging
I dig
and dig
the vines wind
their wicked tendrils
strangling each tender thing
I am trying
to get to the root
then I will pour onto it
whatever poison
might work

SKY BLUE SKY

Draw it
blue pigment
blown
across the page
or seal it
in a bottle
a silk scarf
might float
across
the room
her ghost
beside the bed
taking off
her clothes
skin
goosebumps
sky
the way
the wind
passed through
Emily Dickinson's
window
that afternoon
in August
look
from your sealed
glass height
to feel
the wind
again
try
remember

the color
of the sky
that September
morning
try
remember
the sound

AVERTED VISION

                                                                    Monday

On the soccer field at dusk the children run their laps, talking between heavy breaths. I take a picture.

The tall field lights eclipse the sky.

The soccer dads talk off to one side.

I can not hear what they are saying.

I go back to my car and read a book about traveling, lit by the small overhead light that keeps turning off.

                                                                    Tuesday

Today I wanted to write 1000 lines beginning with the words *what I mean is*.

I wrote nothing.

What I mean is, I am avoiding my feelings.

                                                                 Wednesday

I make a to do list.
I make a grocery list.
I make a list of what the house needs.
I make a list of what my son needs.
I make a list of what the garden needs.
I make a list of the lists I need.

Thursday

I wait for my son.

He is 3D printing robots in a classroom downstairs.

I chose the mountains. Then I chose the hills. I chose boats. Then buses. Then cars. Then crosswalks. Then stop signs. Then overpasses. I'm not a robot.

Friday

The other side of the love poem is the elegy.

Saturday

I choose traffic lights. And more traffic lights. And more traffic lights.

I'm not a robot.

Sunday

It is Sunday.
Upstairs my son practices his clarinet.
Is it okay to have a child? asks one article.
The sound of the Mandalorian march above me.
Fire season did not arrive last year in the fall like it normally does now.
Instead it came in January scorching almost a thousand acres in Big Sur.
Is it okay to have a child? asks a futurist.
What can I help you with? interrupts Siri.
I am two selves at once.
Upstairs my son practices his clarinet.

Monday

Where I am sitting in my car I can see the sun setting in an orange pink fire. I hear the coaches on the field yelling in their low voices. I hear the high-pitched muffled sound of the children.

Tuesday

A woman in front of me in the checkout line has a growth hanging off her arm. It is both her and not her.

I want to stare.

Averted Vision is a technique used by astronomers to view faint objects more clearly utilizing peripheral vision.

Wednesday

Persistence of Vision refers to the phenomenon in which the human perception of the decay of a visual stimulus is slower than the true decay of that stimulus. An image will stay on one's eye for a brief amount of time after its cause has, in reality, disappeared.

Thursday

My son is making robots in his robot class.

I am wandering the museum.

HOW TO DISAPPEAR

In the dead bishop pines beside our house
owls are nesting. At 3 am they call
to one another, which sounds exactly
like someone impersonating two owls
when the moon is full I go outside
and stare into the darkness
to look for them
and again see nothing. Last night
the wind was so strong
I feared the studio we are building
would lift off the ground like a kite.
We had just cut holes in the walls
for windows. It was open
exposed. I had a dream of my mother's house
an excavator had ripped off the door
and cored out the insides. It was all beams
and drifting papers and arguing from within.
A man came out yelling, so I walked away
down River Road, towards nothing.
I have maybe ten photographs of my mother
and also her yearbook, which I took
secretly and never returned. It is off-white
and tattered, with words I never noticed before
on the spine, The Gleam. It smells how an old memory
should smell. Everyone looks the same—
navy blue dresses, Peter Pan collared blouses
I worry I will not recognize her
or will see her and miss her afresh
when I find her in a photograph;
she is sitting with three women
working on the school newspaper
her hair pulled back

her placid smile
she looks at me
I wish I could see her hands.

WINTER GREENS

I plant winter greens
in the cool earth
small seeds of nothing
sprinkled in faint lines
of hope

THE MIRROR STAGE

A young woman stands before a mirror.

A young woman turns away from a full-length wardrobe mirror and then turns back.

She sighs, turns her head from left to right.

She then looks at herself in the mirror.

Half-naked in front of a mirror, she scrutinizes her own body and comments on it out loud.

She traces the lines of her waist.

She looks and looks again.

The daylight blaring at the window, the people in the park, the trees–

The top of the mirror is framed by an elegantly curved ornament.

A young woman stands before a mirror that adorns the door of a wardrobe, carefully examining her body in the reflection.

She has tied up her long dark hair with a hairpin and is wearing nothing but panties bunched around her buttocks.

I have long legs, she notices, and long arms.

She observes herself from the side.

No waist.

A beautiful mouth.

Eyes the same color as my hair.

Scopophilia refers to the derivation of sexual pleasure from looking.

A young woman stands in front of a mirror and submits herself to self-scrutiny, naming body parts, evaluating body parts.

Sensuality is always fraught with ambiguity.

She teases herself because of her belly.

She grabs one wrist with the other hand and clasps it with her fingers. Then switches sides.

She looks and looks again.

There is repetition and circularity in the naming and wording.

She observes herself from the side.

She lets a finger trace the lines of her chin and jaw.

She sighs, turns her head from left to right in small jolts to inspect her body from all angles.

She who seeks shall find.

A young woman stands before a mirror.

This woman does not see herself as beautiful.

The reflection of the body in the mirror.

"A little cellulitis" she says.

Submission to the mirror.

We stand facing this woman who turns her back to us, but whose reflection we are able to see.

Now we see her body from the front, as we look, as she does, at her back.

She looks over her shoulder.

I begin to imagine I am standing in the shadows in her apartment with her, witnessing her solitude like a ghost.

She imagines she is alone.

We follow her inspecting gaze as it travels across her naked flesh.

We appear behind her, literally peering over her shoulder.

If there is a story, it is made by our movement.

She who seeks shall find, find all too well, and end up clouding her vision.

By not gazing at herself, but reflecting instead.

It is more like a window then, to be looked through, than a mirror to reflect back.

A young woman stands before a mirror.

We are aware of every second passing.

The daylight blaring

Watch or don't watch, stay or leave.

I have to get down on my hands and knees to listen to her halting voice coming through the floor.

9PM

Each time a wasp
makes its way through

what should be concrete
walls I have spent the previous hours

telling myself the buzzing
is coming from outside

where in the eaves
the wasps are building a hive

I have been sick
with what has been

coming for me for years
with what is coming for everyone

in bed I listen to the buzzing
and stare at the photograph

that was somehow taken
of what was once the sky

4.6 billion years ago
the world is quiet

the blue light pools
in our eyes

SLEEP SOUND

Every ten seconds there is a beep it is
              the kind of beep one might hear
      if one were in a hospital bed the kind
                  of beep that tells you and everyone

around you you are still alive
              the man with the smile says it is the bay
      the man with the smile then says it is the Bodega Bay
foghorn
                  beeping Bodega Bay is where

Alfred Hitchcock filmed The Birds
              vultures nest in the Cypress grove
      by the beach everywhere there are pictures
                  of Tipi Hedren with her hands

above her head shielding her face
              from the birds Tipi Hedren says things
      like I want to go through life jumping naked
                  into fountains a seagull nicked her

in the head swallows fly down the chimney
              everywhere above us the vultures are
      circling the wind is strong outside
                  and because of the lack of weather

stripping on the door it is howling inside
              every ten seconds the beep
      like a hospital machine beeps in every room
                  there is a sound machine you can hear

the beeping through the white noise also
                through the ocean waves noise and
      through the amazon noise and
                the birds you can't really

hear the beeping through the recorded train noise
              so we turn on the train
          where occasionally the train whistles
                  goodnight! we travel

in our stationary train car
            it is cramped and loud
      I turn off the sound
              it is quiet

I can hear the dust
          particles glistening
      in the sun

BEACH

The water is a type of blue that makes it look like a photograph
                         the water is the type of blue
that makes everyone say   *the water is so blue*
when they see it   and then take a photograph of it

a mother in a green bikini walks back and forth   from the water to
the shore   with her small child   as he fills his bucket full of
the ocean   then dumps it out halfway up the beach
they have been doing this   since we arrived   an hour ago

a sea turtle swims by   then two swim by   everyone
is watching   they bob their heads up and down near the buoy
everyone   is   watching   through   their   phones

my hat makes a waffle pattern over the pages of my green notebook
      it is windy

not everyone I see on the beach is looking down at their phones
       but most are   some are looking into their phones   at
a mirror reflection of themselves taking a photograph of themselves
       one woman with a sunhat on is floating around
on an inner tube in the ocean   face timing her friends

the wind is whistling through my ears   the mother of a
friend of my son arrives   we put sunscreen on our children
      we put sunscreen on ourselves

I know she is about to mention how glad she is   that   we
have coral safe sunscreen   because the non-coral safe
sunscreen is killing the coral   because every time I put
sunscreen on myself or my son someone mentions how sunscreen is
killing the coral   someone always mentions how many more

fish they saw snorkeling twenty years ago   someone
usually mentions garbage island

a pregnant woman walks by in a mauve bikini   her
partner/brother/husband/friend is holding a child   a   baby
maybe she is having another one already   maybe she is still
recovering from having the first one   her belly is round and full
    the baby is asleep

my potential future friend mentions single-use plastics
    then she mentions garbage island

but no one thought to build a wall   the mother of my son's
friend says   no one thought to build a wall   around
the trash on Garbage Island   it drifts and swirls into a vortex that
is now three times the size of France   I nod my head
    thinking about a wall around a soup of trash
    yesterday plastic was found   in human blood
for the first time   she says   I nod my head again
    I nod my head   like a child sent to their room

THERE ARE PLACES WHERE THE SKY COMES CLOSER TO YOU

In the canyon where the plants
have begun to remember
their past lives
    the Currant is again flowering pink sprays
    the Acacia makes soft clouds of yellow disguised as trees
    the dogs have left their footprints like ghosts in the
        hardening ground
the February sky at daybreak is the color of a perfect peach
then submits
to a blue so saturated
  clear, alive, changing—
    my son asks *Why is the sky blue?*
    something about the scattering of light
    I think
    but say *I wonder*

                and think of astronauts
                on the moon facing black skies
                forever in every direction

how they must miss color
how their skin must thirst to drink light
how when they return they must wish to lie prone inside
a sky space
    to be still once again on this blue earth
    to be bathed in the celestial events above

                I feel like an astronaut
                sometimes—now—
                floating far away
                wishing I could walk
                James Turrell's tunnels

where circles become ellipses become apertures
where everything aligns
where you consume light itself—
        is too much light
        just another form
                of blindness?

THERE ARE NO RULES

I don't want to write about how that Helen Frankenthaler painting made me feel. Her big expansive canvas. But I wonder if she got on her knees as she laid her canvas on the ground and poured her turpentine-thinned paint. And did that feel like religion to her? And did she watch with longing as the stain soaked in and became one with the raw canvas? And is this how she thought one day to paint herself into an entire room? And what was that day? Was she in despair? Heartbroken? Was Helen Frankenthaler heartbroken the day she painted herself into an entire room? Did she feel crazed? Possessed? Broken? And did it take her mind off of her pain for a little while, to paint her colors everywhere? Did it let her live inside her painting? And what was it like when Life magazine photographed her?

THE BUTCHER OF PARIS

I drank the last glass
of onomatopoeias
that is done now
the butcher says
while he disembowels
something large
and pink
the blood pools
on the floor
the August sun
shines and shines
the sound of a clock
tick tock in English
tic tac in Spanish
kachi kachi in Japanese
not wanting to write
about something
is not the same
as it does not exist
I can barely hear you
someone says
into their phone
into my phone
I look
I search
for how to say murmur
in another language
an abnormal sound
usually emanating from the heart
that sometimes indicates
a diseased condition
the butcher looks happy

FAILURE FUN HOUSE

I once watched my babysitter, and my babysitter's friend who was not supposed to be there, pour salt into the gas tank of my mother's bright yellow Volvo. They were laughing. I was not. By the laughter and the feeling, the feeling them laughing in the way that makes you know it is wrong, I knew it was wrong. The car never worked again.

~

I poured the xanthum gum down the drain. A birthday cake was in the oven. Jars from the pantry were scattered all over the kitchen counter. It wasn't much. A quarter cup maybe. The sink gurgled the gelatinous goop up onto the floor. And didn't stop. The floor was covered in a thick layer of clear slime. The clog was impenetrable, is what my husband said, is what my father-in-law said, is what the plumber said. I fucked up, is what I thought, and didn't say, and remembered the salt in the gas tank feeling.

~

At lunch the menboys next to us drink sapporo and say fuck every other word behind a plywood makeshift wall that is supposed to protect us somehow from the airborne invisible harm everywhere.

My son points to the chipped orange paint on the wall and wants to leave.

Sometimes holes in the wall are great, I say. And show him a review. He says maybe the owners wrote the review.

Sometimes holes in the wall are great, I say again.

Sometimes holes in the wall are carpenter bees, I think.

My stomach feels off after lunch.

I look pale in the bathroom mirror.

~

It is a little-known fact that carpenter bees hate heavy metal music. My husband plays Iron Maiden in our garage for weeks after seeing them hanging onto our house.

~

Carpenter bees eat houses.

Honey bees live in wax houses.

I live in a wooden house.

I keep honey bees.

I keep honey bees in wooden boxes.

Inside the wooden boxes are frames.

Inside the frames the bees beat their wings in circles to make hexagons.

Inside the hexagons the bees deposit the pollen they collected from the flowers.

Inside the box, inside the frames, inside the prismatic pollen rainbows, somewhere is the queen.

Inside the queen are her eggs.

The queen lays fifteen hundred eggs a day.

One day the queen lays a different egg.

The queen makes another queen.

~

The original queen leaves.

And takes half her hive with her.

To find another home.

~

A disparate grey black buzzing cloud consumes my entire street.

~

I walk outside in my white suite of seemingly no protection and tell myself I am not afraid.

~

Vibration is not a sound. It is a feeling.

~

I reach up into the three-foot dense ball of undulating black and white and yellow vibration.

~

I am not afraid.

~

I am sorry for interrupting whatever you would have been doing right now, I say to the retired police officer holding my ladder. It's okay, he says. I was just going hunting, he says.

What do you hunt, I ask.

My favorite thing to hunt is people, he says. Laughing.

What kind of people, I ask. Laughing.

The worst kind, he says.

And I know what he means.

And so do you.

~

I clip the branch and the entire buzzing ball falls into the box below in a loud sound.

~

What I wanted to say to him was that my mother's boyfriend was the worst kind.

~

I write about my mother's boyfriend in a poem.

I delete every I.

Then I delete every him.

Then I delete the poem.

~

The stray drones search for the queen, landing on the box, scaling its sides, frantically searching for the small doorway inside to protect her.

~

By nightfall, they are gone.

~

I delete the poem.

GLASS CONCERT

When I was six my older brother took my doll out of
her   doll   bed   and   ran
around   the   house
I   chased   him
watching   the   top of her head   bobbing
in   his.   arms   as   he   ran
s   c   r   e   a   m   i   n   g
I   could   not   keep   up
he   ran and ran and   ran
outside   around   the   house   then   back
through   the   front   door
which slammed   behind   him
I   could   not   stop
I   crashed   through
with   my   hands   in   front   of   me
what   was   solid
became   the   breaking   sound
a   lot   of   glass
a   lot   of   blood
my   mother   was not   home
she   had   said
do   not   leave   the   house
and   I   had
later much later   maybe only now   as I write these
words   believe   she   must   have   been
at   the   liquor   store
maybe   the   grocery   store but   most   likely
the   liquor   store
Mrs.   North
a   nurse   across   the   street
saw   me   sitting   on   my   front   stoop
in   the   middle   of
the mess   of   glass and blood
she   said   she had   butterfly   band-aids   at home

which			sounded			pretty
which		made		me		smile
which			turned			out
to	neither	have	butterflies		on	them
nor	look	like	butterflies		at	all
she		covered	me		in	them

A PLACE

He found a place
in her heart

I am tired of this place
he once said

only in jest
but I am tired of this place

took up residence too
and then they were both

living in her heart
he also had a place

in the mountains
where he would go

sometimes. This place
in the mountains

was also in her heart
in a different way

at times she would think
about the place in the mountains

in her heart with great feeling
staring longingly off

years passed and still
he had a place in her heart

no matter where she went
his place in her heart

went with her
and so did his I am tired

of this place
and also his place

in the mountains
of her heart

in this way
she was never alone

I AM NOT WRITING AN INSTAGRAM POST

I am not writing a Facebook status update. I am not writing a tweet. I am not writing a thank-you card. I am not writing an apology email. I am not writing a lyric essay. I am not writing a scientific paper. I am not writing a poem. I am not writing about contemporary art. I am not writing about my summer travels. I am not writing about how 5,200 tons of stardust falls to earth each year. I am not writing about how you age faster at the top of mountains, but more slowly in space. I am not writing about the origin of witches. I am not writing about sonic pollution. I am not writing about the beauty of fog. I am not writing about the figure in contemporary painting. I am not writing about porn addiction. I am not writing about the increasing rate of suicide. I am not writing about the movement of the tectonic plates. I am not writing about the history of the haunted house. I am not writing about digestion. I am not writing about performance art. I am not writing about longing. I am not writing about grief. I am not writing about midlife. I am not writing about shame. I am not writing about eavesdropping. I am not writing about the color gray. I am not writing about negative space. I am not writing about absence. I am not writing about disappearance. I am not writing about my mother.

THE ATTIC

In the attic
I feel a little sad

I may feel a little sad
downstairs too

but I notice the little sadness most
in the attic

WALKING DOWN CHURCH STREET AT 5PM ON A MONDAY

by atmosphere I mean
I walk home

from the market
and watch a man

holding a watermelon
in one palm

high up
near his head

his body
is shadows

long gray lines
walking across pavement

LIVING ROOM

It is night. It is too hot to sleep in my bed. So I go downstairs and lie on the floor of the living room where it is cooler. My son also comes down and lies on the floor of the living room. I try to sleep. It is still too hot. I hear his feet moving on the carpet. I tell him to sleep. I also tell myself to sleep. Goodnight I say, to both of us. One time, when I was a camp counselor, I left my car keys in the lake house. The lake was down a long path in the woods, far away from the art yurt where I was. It was dark. I walked with only the light of the moon. The moon and the fireflies. And the sound of the leaves beneath my feet. And the din of the crickets. I was hoping this memory would lead me somewhere. But it is still night and it is still hot and it is still dark and I still can't sleep. I could say that I was on the path in the dark with the moon and the fireflies trying, as always, to forget my way.

EARLY MORNING SOUNDS

a group of little girls
half-hidden by fog
jumping rope
singing

DAGUERROTYPE

Wandering Rue Daguerre
looking for Agnes Varda's ghost

I do not know what I expected
to find. I wanted

to walk the sidewalks
she walked. I wanted to see

the buildings she saw. May we
try, may we try, I ask in French

at the ice cream shop
Yes, yes, she says. You may

try, she says
in French and stares

at me and my son,
who are staring

at the ice cream. I do not
know what I expected

to find. Perhaps I did
not wander

far enough

REBELLION IN SILENCE

He cleared a space within her
she had not known to be crowded
just as when alone
in her backyard reading
she shuddered
when an unkindness of ravens
scattered suddenly
into the stone sky
wild black flapping
a mess of noise
she wondered how
she had not noticed
birds that large
and so many

SKY BURIAL

So close to sleep, I might be
still dreaming, in a soft blur of thoughts
I think of the skatepark from above
smears of color where the children were
etched into the air. The sky
up here where I sit in my dream sight
fills me with the sensation of the color
blue. As a child, my favorite book
was the Rainbow Goblins. Blue
was an angry goblin. He sucked
all of the color out of the sky. A colorless
sky remained. When my mother died
she did not have much. Three heavy white
bankers boxes arrived on my doorstep.
I wanted to roll out a field of sunprint paper
and on it place each object, each thrift store
trinket, what remained. I wanted to watch
the sun burn in a memory of them
bury them in the light

A LOT OF SORROW

I definitely did not
sit for six hours
listening to sorrow
I am as afraid
of whatever
that would do to me
as I am afraid
of Ayahuasca
maybe it is sublime
the feeling
this is not sustainable
but will have to be
is everywhere
a kind of melancholic
stage light gel
through which
somehow
we keep living

NOTES

Jawbreaker, On *Jawbreaker*, performative video piece by Andrew Simsak and Cynthia Randolph made with footage from an eight and a half hour performance, 2005.

Sound Effects, Erasure poem of sound directions from the script of Wes Craven's 1984 horror movie, *Nightmare on Elm Street*.

Wings, On *Wing* by Elizabeth Turk, 1996 and *Spider* by Louise Bourgeois, 1995.

Rome, On *100 Years* by Hans-Peter Feldmann, MAXXI, Museo Nationale delle arti dei XXI secolo, 2001.

A Walk in the Woods is an erasure of Bob Ross, Joy of Painting, Episode 1, *A Walk in the Woods*, 1983.

Every Day I Miss the Sunset so I Turn Away from the Sky, On Mysteries of the Horizon, by René Magritte,1955.

In the Museum of Hunting and Nature, references Pleureuse, by Serena Carone, exhibited in the Musée de la Chasse et de la Nature in Paris in 2017, alongside an exhibition by the artist Sophie Calle where she took over the entire museum, installing artworks on all its floors in dialogue with the permanent collection.

Josef Albers, Homage to the Square: Guarded, 1952, On *Homage to the Square: Guarded* by Josef Albers, 1952, Titles of Albers' other works are threaded throughout this piece.

An Impossible Thing is Happening in the Most Boring Place You Can Imagine, "There is special providence in the fall of a sparrow" is from *Hamlet,* Act 5, Scene 2, by William Shakespeare.

There are Places Where the Sky Comes Closer to You, On *Roden Crater* by James Turrell, Ongoing.

There are No Rules, On *Beyond the Sea,* by Helen Frankenthaler, *1952.*

I Am Not Writing an Instagram Post*,* "I am not writing" is a line taken from a piece by Ann Boyer, *Not Writing,* from her book Garments Against Women.

Green Light Corridor*,* On *Green Light Corridor,* by Bruce Nauman, 1970

Sky Blue Sky*,* On *Wind (through Emily Dickinson's window, August 14, 2012, 3:22 pm),* by Spencer Finch.

The Mirror Stage*,* The lines in this poem have been taken and collaged from art reviews of *In the Mirror,* by the artist and filmmaker Chantal Ackerman. *In the Mirror* is a video work Ackerman created using footage from her film *L'enfant aime – ou je joue a etre une femme mariee (The Beloved Child, or I Play at Being a Married Woman*), 1971. The scene itself lasts 14 minutes and 21 seconds, though in her video work the scene is looped, and therefore an endless meditation on the scene of a woman standing before a mirror examining her own body.

Sleep Sound*, The Birds* is a 1963 natural horror-thriller directed by Alfred Hitchcock and filmed in Bodega Bay, California. The movie is based loosely on a short story of the same name by Daphne du Maurier, written in 1952.

Early Morning Sounds is an erasure poem of sound directions from the script of Wes Craven's 1984 horror movie, *Nightmare on Elm Street.*

Daguerreotype*,* Agnes Varda lived on Rue Daguerre, a street in Paris, for several decades. In her 1975 documentary film, *Daguerréotypes,* Varda wanders her own street taking video portraits of shop owners. Her son was two at the time, prohibiting her from wandering far from her house for her art, so she spent what little time she had, often while her son was napping, close to home, sometimes snaking an extension cord through her mail slot so she could film the people around her, asking each shop owner the same three questions "*Where did you come from?*", "*When did you get here?*", "*Why did you come?*" And while the name of her actual street was Rue Daguerre, the film also references Louis Daguerre, who invented the method of photographic printing known as the Daguerreotype.

Rebellion in Silence, Title is from Rebecca Horn's exhibition *Rebellion in Silence: Dialogue Between Raven and Whale,* 2009.

A Lot of Sorrow, On Ragnar Kjartansson's six-hour durational performance piece, *A Lot of Sorrow*, in collaboration with the band The National at MoMA PS1, NYC, 2013. Kjartansson asked the band to perform their song *A Lot of Sorrow* repeatedly for six hours. The video piece that resulted from this performance has been exhibited in numerous museums.

AUTHOR'S NOTE

I titled this collection of poems *In the Museum of Hunting and Nature*, as this book works in a similar way to the museum in Paris of the same name, which is a museum of inclusion and maximalism, often juxtaposing one style, age, or medium, right up next to another, in order to create a new dialogue between them. Hunting equipment, trophies, taxidermy, as well as ancient, modern, and contemporary art, are all exhibited side by side. The result is a museum that feels alive, and maybe too, close to real life which, of course, is never one thing, never one theme. Often the exhibits have the feel of a kind of cabinet of curiosities. Some are fantastical in nature, such as one cabinet which is dedicated entirely to unicorns. In a similar way, this book houses a varied collection of poems, ranging formally, as well as thematically, from poems which reference modern and contemporary art, to poems which explore our relationship with the natural world, as well as our inherent nature. When faced with decisions about which poems to include in this book, as well as how to arrange them, I thought about how the Museum of Hunting and Nature curates its collections, then used that as a kind of ghost scaffold. I allowed my intuition to place what might seem like unlikely poems next to one another, but which belong together. Through this mysterious process, the poems taught me what they are. And I listened. I am still listening.

ACKNOWLEDGEMENTS

Tremendous gratitude for the incredibly talented writers who read these poems in their tenderest beginnings, sometimes before they were even poems. Thank you to Jane Barnard, Jill Brooks, Michele Ferrari, Ruth Goldberg, Margaux Kent, Monika Sengul-Jones, Deborah Stein, and Dorothy Woodhouse. I know my writing, and my life, would be so much less without your friendship, and our community. I am certain many of these poems would never fully exist without you. Immeasurable gratitude for the magic that is Sabrina Orah Mark. I don't know how I would have navigated these last three and half years without our conversations about writing, which of course are conversations about living. Thank you to Cole Swensen for your meticulous eye, and ear, and heart. Thank you to Matthew Zapruder, Sara Mumolo, Kaveh Akbar, Mark Wunderlich, Joseph Lease, Matthew Dickman, Brenda Hillman, Robert Hass, and everyone at the Community of Writers for living lives in poetry, reading my work, sharing your insights, you passion, and your support. And while Mary Ruefle has not read a single one of these poems (yet!), it would be remiss not to thank her for her words, which haunt me often.

Thank you to the artists mentioned in these poems, and their work, to which I return again and again, for the life they breathe back into me when I have needed it most. Thank you especially to Elizabeth Turk, for your art, your couch all those years ago, and your friendship.

Thank you to my father and stepmother, for instilling in me, and sharing with me, a love of language. Thank you to Michelle Gannon for everything you do. Thank you to Nathalie and Marty for your constant love and support. Thank you to the Eigs, all of you, always.

Thank you to Tamsin Smith and Matt Gonzalez for publishing this collection and believing in it, and me. Thank you to the editors of the publications where some of these poems first appeared: *Sky Blue Sky*, Omniverse Issue 86, 2020; *Sky Burial*, Community of

Writers Poetry Review, 2021; *How to Disappear*, Odes To Our Undoing, 2022, Risk Press.

Finally, thank you to my first readers, my truest loves, Andrew and Loden, for our family. I could not have done this, and continue to do this, without you. These poems would not be what they are without you. I would not be who I am without you. I love you with everything I have.

—

A farmer told me recently to always give back a little more than you take from the earth, and also from life. I might bury this book in my garden, following in the footsteps of Mary Ruefle and W. S. Merwin, and others. Maybe a tree will grow, nourished by these poems, which I am now imagining being eaten by worms and bugs and the microbiome. And maybe the tree that grows will be a fruit tree. And maybe I will make a pie from the fruit of the poem tree. And maybe I will bring it (somehow!) to eat with everyone listed here, and also everyone who is not listed, but should also be acknowledged, including you. And maybe we will sit someplace in the warm shade and eat it together, and then the fruit and the poems and the microbiome will live inside of us all, for a little while.

Cynthia Randolph, 2018

Cynthia Randolph is an artist and writer who works across photography, video, poetry, and creative nonfiction. She has received a Vermont Studio Center Artist Grant, George B. Hill and Therese Muller Creative Writing Awards, and has exhibited throughout the United States and abroad. Her writing has been published in *Canvas, Omniverse, Written Here (and There), The Community of Writers Poetry Review 2020,* and *Odes to Our Undoing: Poets Processing Crisis, An Anthology (Risk Press, 2022)*. She earned an MFA in Sculpture from Cranbrook Academy of Art, an MBA in Design Strategy from California College of the Arts, and a BS in English Literature and Creative Writing from the University of Wisconsin-Madison. She lives in San Francisco with her husband and son.

THE PAGE POETS SERIES

Number 1
Between First & Second Sleep by Tamsin Spencer Smith

Number 2
The Michaux Notebook by Micah Ballard

Number 3
Sketch of the Artist by Patrick James Dunagan

Number 4
Different Darknesses by Jason Morris

Number 5
Suspension of Mirrors by Mary Julia Klimenko

Number 6
The Rise & Fall of Johnny Volume by Garrett Caples

Number 7
Used with Permission by Charlie Pendergast

Number 8
Deconfliction by Katharine Harer

Number 9
Unlikely Saviors by Stan Stone

Number 10
Beauty Will Be Convulsive by Matt Gonzalez

Number 11
Displacement Geology by Tamsin Spencer Smith

Number 12
The Public Sound by Marina Lazzara

Number 13
Record of Records by Rod Roland

Number 14
Strangers We Have Known by John Briscoe

Number 15
Cutting Teeth by Jesse Holwitz

Number 16
Other Scavengers by Lauren Caldwell

Number 17
In the Museum of Hunting and Nature by Cynthia Randolph

Made in United States
Troutdale, OR
06/01/2023